Japanese
favorites

Features all the classic Japanese recipes like
Miso Soup with Clams, Braised Daikon, Udon
Noodle Soup with Tempura and Pork Cutlet with
Egg on Rice (Tonkatsu).

PERIPLUS

Basic Japanese Ingredients

Agar-agar or *kanten* is a gelatin-like thickener that is made from seaweed. It is used like gelatin to make jellies and moulded desserts. It melts at a higher temperature than gelatin, which makes it suitable for use in hot climates, and produces a more delicate and firm texture than gelatin. Store in a cool, dry place. It is available in powdered form or as long, dried strips in packets.

Azuki beans are small, red beans that look like tiny kidney beans. They are sold dried or in tins in supermarkets. Dried azuki beans should be soaked overnight in water then cooked until tender. The canned beans may be used straight from the tin.

Basil is available in several varieties, each with a different scent. Fresh Asian basil is used in many Asian dishes. If fresh basil is not available, the best substitute is sweet basil or fresh coriander leaves or mint as dried basil does not have the same flavor. Basil is available fresh in markets and the refrigerator sections of supermarkets.

Bonito flakes are shavings of dried, smoked and cured bonito fish, sold in fine or coarse flakes in small plastic packs. Fine flakes are used as a garnish, while coarse flakes are used to make *dashi* fish stock. Store unused portions in an airtight container.

Burdock is a long, slender root that is rich in fiber and nutrients. It should be scraped and not peeled before use as much of its flavor is close to the skin. Substitute with French beans.

Daikon is a large, white radish widely used in Japanese cooking. It may be eaten raw or cooked and is often pickled or grated. Used mainly in soups and stir-fries, it is sold in supermarkets.

Dashi powder is used to make *dashi* fish stock and as a basic seasoning in many soups and salad dressings. It may be substituted with soup stock powder or bouillon cubes.

Dried green seaweed flakes or *aonori*, are sold in small bottles in supermarkets and used as a garnish in various fried noodle dishes.

Japanese cucumbers are smaller, thinner and sweeter than normal cucumbers and have much smaller seeds. Since they are rarely available outside Japan, we have substituted baby cucumbers. Pickling cucumbers or gherkins may also be used.

Japanese eggplants are long and narrow with sweet, tender flesh. They should be rubbed briskly with salt or rinsed with salt water after cutting to prevent discoloration.

Japanese mustard is hotter than French or English mustard. It is made from a blend of ground mustard seeds without the addition of flour. Japanese mustard is sold in powdered form in small tins or as a paste in tubes and is available in supermarkets.

Japanese mayonnaise is thicker, creamier and saltier than Western mayonnaise, however Western mayonnaise may be used as a substitute. Japanese mayonnaise is sold in small bottles.

Japanese rice is a short-grain variety that is slightly more starchy than Thai or Chinese long-grain rice. Available from most supermarkets, it may be substituted with any short- or medium-grain rice.

Japanese sesame oil is milder than Chinese sesame oil. If not available, substitute by diluting 1 part Chinese sesame oil with 1 part vegetable oil.

Japanese turnips are protein- and calcium-rich tubers that are widely used in Japanese cooking. The roots and sometimes leaves are often used in pickles. Japanese turnips are available in wet markets and supermarkets.

Konnyaku is a dark jelly made from a root vegetable similar to taro, known as "devil's tongue". It is usually sold in powdered form in packets. It is sometimes available in blocks or thin strips in sealed plastic packets, and is generally used to add texture to dishes.

Leeks used in Asian cooking are smaller and more delicate than European leeks. If leeks are not available, substitute with spring onions or European leeks.

Lotus root is the thick tuber of the aquatic lotus plant and is available fresh in supermarkets. It is sold either covered in mud or cleaned and wrapped in plastic. A good substitute is jicama (*bangkuang*) or cauliflower.

Mirin is a sweet liquid made by mixing and fermenting steamed glutinous rice with *shoju* (a distilled spirit similar to vodka). It adds a lovely glaze to grilled foods and is used to flavor soup stocks, marinades and dressings.

Miso is a fermented paste made from soybeans and wheat. **Red miso paste** is red to brown in color, high in protein and more salty than **white miso paste**, which is sweeter and milder. Miso is used to enhance the flavor of soups, stocks and dressings, and as a grilling baste for meats and fish. Never boil miso as it will curdle and lose its flavor.

Mitsuba is a herb used in some soups and salads. It is often added to dishes as a garnish. *Mitsuba* stalks may be tied, dipped in batter, and deep-fried as tempura. It tastes similar to celery leaves and is sold in the refrigerator sections of supermarkets. It may be substituted with chervil.

Mushrooms are a vital ingredient in Japanese cuisine. **Shiitake mushrooms** are large and meaty, and used in soups, stir-fries and side dishes, or as a meat substitute. Dried Chinese mushroooms are a good substitute. **Enoki mushrooms** are clusters of slender, cream-colored stalks with tiny caps, available fresh or in cans. Discard the tough ends of the *enoki* mushroom before use.

Noodles come in many different sizes and shapes in Japan. **Udon noodles** are made from wheat, and are either flat or round but generally quite thick. Packets of whitish-beige dried *udon* are available in supermarkets. **Soba noodles** are made from buckwheat, and are sometimes flavored with green tea. While *soba* noodles are available fresh in Japan, they are usually available only in dried form outside Japan.

Nori is a type of seaweed pressed into very thin sheets and baked (*yaki nori*) or seasoned with sweetened soy sauce (*ajitsuke nori*). It is sold in rectangular sheets packed in bundles of 10. *Yaki nori* is used for making sushi rolls, while *ajitsuke nori* is served with rice or crisps as an appetizer. Before use, wave a *nori* sheet over an open flame for a few seconds so that it becomes lightly toasted, or toast briefly in a toaster oven.

Pickled apricots or *umeboshi* are soaked in salt or brine, then dried in the sun. Red shiso leaves are often added during the pickling process to color the apricots. Pickled apricots are sold in jars or packets in supermarkets.

Potato starch is similar to cornflour but is more readily dissolved in liquid without becoming lumpy. Cornflour is a good substitute, however.

Red pickled ginger is made by pickling ginger slices first in salt, then in vinegar. This pickling process gives the ginger its distinctive color. It is sold in jars and used as a garnish.

Rice wine vinegar is slightly sweeter and milder than cider or wine vinegars. It is used in making sushi rice, in dressings and as a basic seasoning. It may be substituted with apple cider vinegar.

Sake is a brewed alcoholic beverage also known as Japanese rice wine. Chinese rice wine or sherry may be used as a substitute.

Sesame seeds are available in black and white varieties, although white seeds are more common. White sesame seeds are toasted and crushed to make sesame paste.

Seven-spice pepper powder or *shichimi togarashi* generally includes a combination of: black pepper, red chili pepper, sesame seeds, green nori seaweed flakes, dried orange peels, prickly ash pods and poppy seeds. It is sprinkled on noodles, one-pot meals and grilled items.

Shiso leaves are large, flat green or reddish-green leaves that have a flavor similar to basil, mint and spearmint. Fresh basil, or a mix of fresh basil and spearmint, are the closest substitutes.

Soy sauce is brewed from wheat, salt and soy beans. **Dark soy sauce** gives a slightly "smokey" flavor to a dish,

while **regular soy sauce** is thinner and saltier. If Japanese soy sauce is unavailable, use Chinese soy sauce.

Tempura flour or *tempura ko*, generally contains cornstarch, baking powder and wheat flour. It is mixed with eggs, wheat flour and water to form a batter and is available as a powder sealed in foil or plastic packets in supermarkets. If tempura flour is not available, substitute $1/2$ cup cornstarch mixed with $1/2$ cup wheat flour

Tofu is a protein-rich food made from soy beans. It is sold packed in sealed plastic tubs or small plastic bags in the refrigerator sections of supermarkets. Tofu can vary greatly in firmness and flavor, and it is important to purchase the correct type called for in the recipes. **Firm tofu** retains its shape when sliced or cooked and has a slightly sour taste. **Silken tofu**, or soft tofu, is slippery and extremely soft. It crumbles easily but has a smoother texture and milder flavor than firm tofu.

Tonkatsu sauce is eaten with Japanese-style pork cutlets. It tastes similar to steak sauce and usually contains Worcestershire sauce, tomato ketchup, soy sauce, mustard and sake. It is available in bottles in supermarkets. Steak sauce may be substituted.

Wakame seaweed is sold dried in strips. Dried *wakame* is light brown and should be soaked in water before use. It is often added to soups, a few minutes before serving and has a crunchy texture. This calcium-rich seaweed may also be toasted and crumbled over soups and other dishes.

Dashi Stock

1 1/2 liters (6 cups)
  water
3 tablespoons dried
  bonito flakes
3 dried *shiitake* mush-
  rooms, thinly sliced
2 1/2-cm (2-in) length of
  konbu seaweed, thor-
  oughly washed

Makes about 1 1/2 liters
  (6 cups) of stock
Preparation time: **5 mins**
Cooking time: **15 mins**

1 Place water, dried bonito flakes, mushrooms and *konbu* into a saucepan and bring to a boil. Reduce heat and simmer uncovered for 10 minutes or until bonito flakes sink to the bottom.

2 Drain stock and set aside to cool. Store cooled Dashi Stock in the refrigerator until use, for not more than 3 days. Dashi Stock is used in the recipes for Classic Miso Soup with Tofu on page 6 and Braised Daikon on page 20.

Tempura Batter

1 egg, lightly beaten
3/4 cup (190 ml) iced
  water, adding extra as
  needed
1 cup tempura flour or
  1/2 cup cornstarch
  mixed with 1/2 cup
  flour

Preparation time: **5 mins**

1 To make the Tempura Batter, combine the egg and iced water in a bowl. Sprinkle half of the tempura flour over the top and whisk. Add remaining tempura flour and mix until almost combined. The batter should still be a little lumpy. Tempura Batter is used in the recipes for Udon Noodles in Soup with Prawn and Vegetable Tempura Fritters on page 49 and Tempura Rice Broth on page 59.

If the Tempura Batter settles while you are preparing the food, a new batch of batter must be made, since batter that has settled does not yield crispy tempura. Therefore, try to prepare the tempura batter at the last minute, after all the other tempura ingredients are prepared and ready for frying.

Classic Miso Soup with Tofu

5 teaspoons *dashi* powder dissolved in 750 ml (3 cups) water or 750 ml (3 cups) Dashi Stock (see page 5)
2 tablespoons dried *wakame* seaweed, torn
4 tablespoons red miso paste
150 g (5 oz) silken tofu, cubed
1 tablespoon thinly sliced spring onions, to garnish
10–12 pickled apricots, to serve (optional)

Serves 4
Preparation time: **10 mins**
Cooking time: **8 mins**

1 Place *dashi* mixture or Dashi Stock into a medium saucepan and bring to the boil. Remove from the heat and sprinkle with the dried *wakame* seaweed.
2 Place the miso paste into a small bowl and stir in a little of the stock liquid until the paste is of pouring consistency. Gradually stir into the soup stock and add the cubed tofu.
3 Ladle into 4 individual bowls, garnish with spring onions and serve with pickled apricots, if desired.

The soup may be prepared ahead of time and kept for up to 5 days in a sealed container in the refrigerator. Do not let the soup boil or the miso will curdle and lose its flavor. Add spring onions just before serving.

Tuna and Leek Salad

2 tablespoons thinly sliced leeks
1 baby cucumber (about 100 g/3$^1/_2$ oz), washed
2 fresh shiso or large basil leaves, shredded
1$^1/_2$ teaspoons grated ginger
400 g (14 oz) fresh sashimi-quality tuna
Black sesame seeds, (optional)

Ginger Dipping Sauce
1$^1/_2$ teaspoons grated ginger
$^1/_2$ teaspoon dark soy sauce

1 Place the leeks in a small bowl of cold water and soak for 5 minutes. Drain and pat dry with paper towels. Shred the cucumber into long, thin strips and set aside.
2 Combine the sliced leeks and shredded shiso or basil leaves in a small bowl. Add half of the grated ginger and toss well to combine. Dice the tuna and combine with the leek mixture.
3 To prepare the Ginger Dipping Sauce, divide the ginger between 4 small sauce bowls and top with dark soy sauce to taste.
4 Divide the tuna mixture into 4 equal portions. Place each portion on a serving dish. Sprinkle with black sesame seeds, if desired. Garnish with the reserved shredded cucumber and serve with the Ginger Dipping Sauce on the side.

Serves 4
Preparation time: **12–15 mins**

Mixed Japanese Pickles

150 g (5 oz) daikon

80 g (3 oz) lotus root, peeled

150 g (5 oz) Japanese turnip, diced (about 1 cup)

2 tablespoons rice wine vinegar

2 tablespoons salt

2 baby cucumbers (about 85 g/3 oz each)

8 fresh *shiitake* mushrooms, stalks removed and cut into bite-sized pieces

4 teaspoons peeled and grated fresh ginger

4 fresh shiso leaves, shredded

5 tablespoons soy sauce

2 tablespoons *mirin*

2 teaspoons sesame oil

Serves 6
Preparation time: 20 mins
  + 6–7 hours standing

1 Remove the skin and thick outer layer of daikon. Cut daikon and lotus root into bite-sized pieces. Place daikon, lotus root, turnip and vinegar in a bowl of cold water for 10 minutes.

2 Meanwhile, sprinkle a chopping board with 1 teaspoon of the salt and slowly roll the cucumbers back and forth over the salt. Cut into quarters lengthwise and slice thinly.

3 Drain the daikon, lotus and turnip, pat dry with a paper towel and place in a large bowl with mushrooms and cucumber. Sprinkle with remaining salt, cover with a sheet of plastic wrap or waxed paper and place a heavy weight on top to press the vegetables down. Set aside to stand for 1 hour.

4 Wash thoroughly under cold water, pat dry with a paper towel and combine in a large bowl with ginger, shiso, soy sauce, *mirin* and sesame oil. Toss well to coat and set aside to stand in a cool, dry place for 5–6 hours or overnight. Pickles will keep up to 1 month in the refrigerator.

Dried Chinese mushrooms may be used instead of fresh shiitake *mushrooms. Soak the dried mushrooms in warm water for 10–15 minutes to soften, remove and discard stalks.*

Omelet Roll with Fish (Datemaki)

40 g (¹/₂ cup) uncooked white, soft-fleshed fish, sliced
1 teaspoon rice wine vinegar
6 eggs
¹/₂ teaspoon *dashi* powder dissolved in ¹/₃ cup (80 ml) water
¹/₃ cup sugar
2 teaspoons soy sauce
¹/₂ teaspoon salt
1 teaspoon oil

Serves 4–6
Preparation time: 20 mins + 25 mins cooling
Cooking time: 20 mins

1 Place the fish and vinegar in a blender or mortar and pestle and process or pound to form a thick paste. Place the fish paste into a medium bowl and slowly beat in the white of one egg, reserving the egg yolk. When the egg white is incorporated, mix in the reserved egg yolk. Slowly beat in the remaining eggs, one at a time, until well combined. Do not allow the egg mixture to foam.

2 Combine the *dashi* mixture, sugar, soy sauce and salt in a bowl and carefully stir into egg mixture. Heat the oil in a frying pan over medium heat. Add the egg mixture, then reduce heat to very low. Cook for 20 minutes or until the top of the omelet is dry. Swirl the pan to evenly brown the bottom of the omelet. When cooked, carefully turn the omelet over and cook the other side for 1 minute over low heat until lightly browned.

3 Place the omelet on a bamboo rolling mat. Fold over the first 5 cm (2 in) of the omelet and press down gently with the mat. Lift the mat away from the omelet and continue rolling the omelet. Secure the mat around the rolled omelet with elastic bands and set aside for 25–30 minutes, or until cool. Carefully unroll the mat, slice the omelet roll into 1¹/₂-cm (¹/₂-in) pieces and serve.

Place the omelet on a bamboo rolling mat.

Fold over the first 5 cm (2 in) of the omelet and press down gently with the mat.

Lift the mat and continue rolling the omelet.

Secure the mat around the rolled omelet and set aside for 25–30 minutes, or until cool.

Sautéed Eggplant

5 Japanese eggplants
  (about 400 g/14 oz)
4 tablespoons oil
$^1/_2$ small red chili, thinly
  sliced
2 tablespoons red miso
  paste
4 teaspoons sugar
2 teaspoons soy sauce
1 tablespoon water
2 teaspoons toasted
  white sesame seeds
  (optional)
Few sprigs parsley, to
  garnish (optional)

1 Peel 4 lengthwise strips of skin from each eggplant in alternating strips and discard. Slice each eggplant into $2^1/_2$-cm (1-in) rounds.

2 Place the eggplants in a bowl of cold water for 10 minutes. Drain and pat dry on a paper towel.

3 Heat the oil in a saucepan over medium heat. Add the eggplants and stir-fry for 5 minutes or until tender. Add chili, miso, sugar, soy sauce and water and stir-fry for 30 seconds. Sprinkle with sesame seeds, if desired, and serve warm.

Serves 4
Preparation time: 10 mins
Cooking time: 8 mins

Prawns Cooked in Sake and Mirin

12 medium prawns
(about 350 g/12 oz)
4 small bamboo skewers
160 ml (²/₃ cup) sake
4 teaspoons *mirin*
4 teaspoons soy sauce
2 very thin lemon slices,
quartered, to garnish
(optional)

Serves 4
Preparation time:
8–10 mins
Cooking time: **10 mins**

1 Peel and devein prawns leaving heads and tails intact. Thread 3 prawns onto each skewer keeping the tail and head close together, then set aside.

2 Place the sake, *mirin* and soy sauce in a medium saucepan and bring to a boil. Reduce heat to low and cook prawns, two skewers at a time, for about 2 minutes or until pink and cooked through.

3 Remove skewers from saucepan and set aside. Increase heat to high and bring the sake mixture to a boil. Reduce heat to medium and simmer until thick and syrupy. Remove from the heat.

4 Place skewered prawns on serving plates and drizzle sauce over them. Garnish with lemon slices, if desired, and serve.

Miso Soup with Clams

150 g (5 oz) baby clams
1 liter (4 cups) water
4 dried *shiitake* or Chinese mushrooms, sliced
2 teaspoons *dashi* powder
5-cm (2-in) strip of *nori*, washed thoroughly
$3^1/_2$ tablespoons red miso paste
Few sprigs Japanese *mitsuba* or chervil, to garnish

1 Place the clams in a basin, scrub with a brush to clean, then rinse. Soak the clams in cold water for 10 minutes. Drain, rinse well and set aside.
2 Meanwhile, place the water in a large saucepan and bring to a boil. Add the mushrooms, *dashi* powder and *nori*, reduce heat to low and simmer for 15 minutes covered. Increase heat to medium, add clams and cook for 2–3 minutes covered or until shells open slightly, discarding any that do not open. Remove pan from heat and discard the mushrooms.
3 Divide clams into 4 serving bowls using a slotted spoon. Place miso paste into another small bowl and stir in a little of the soup stock until the paste is of pouring consistency. Gradually stir the miso mixture into the soup stock.
4 To serve, pour miso soup over the top of the clams and garnish with sprigs of *mitsuba* or chervil.

Serves 4
Preparation time: **10 mins**
Cooking time: **25–30 mins**

Pickled White Radish with Chili

1 red chili
100 g (3 ¹/₂ oz) daikon
1 teaspoon salt

Serves 4
Preparation time: 6 mins
  + 2 days standing

1 Remove the seeds from the chili and slice into very thin strips.
2 Remove skin and thick outer layer of daikon. Cut in half and then slice thinly.
3 Place daikon and chili in a large bowl, sprinkle with salt and toss to combine.
4 Cover with a sheet of plastic wrap or waxed paper and place a heavy weight on top to press the vegetables down. Let stand for 2 days in the refrigerator. Wash thoroughly under cold water to remove excess salt before serving.

Cold Tofu Appetizer

2 tablespoons thinly sliced leek
300 g (10 oz) silken tofu
2 teaspoons freshly grated ginger
2–3 tablespoons soy sauce
2–3 teaspoons dried bonito flakes

1 Soak the leeks in a small bowl of cold water for 10 minutes and drain. Drain tofu and pat dry on paper towels. Cut the tofu block into 4 equal pieces. Carefully divide tofu between 4 small bowls.
2 Divide the ginger and leek into 4 equal portions and place on top of tofu. Drizzle over the soy sauce and serve with bonito flakes on the side.

Serves 4
Preparation time: 15 mins

Hot Silken Tofu in Soy Broth

300 g (10 oz) silken tofu
2 sheets *nori*
1 stalk spring onions, shredded, soaked in iced water and drained, to garnish
2 teaspoons grated ginger, to garnish

Soy Dipping Sauce
$1/_4$ teaspoon *dashi* powder dissolved in 2 tablespoons water
3 tablespoons soy sauce
2 tablespoons *mirin*

Miso Dipping Sauce
$1/_2$ tablespoon white miso paste
$1/_2$ tablespoon red miso paste
2 teaspoons rice wine vinegar
$1/_2$ teaspoon of salt
$1/_2$ tablespoon sugar
$1/_2$ tablespoon soy sauce
$1/_2$ tablespoon *mirin*

1 Combine the Soy Dipping Sauce ingredients in a small bowl and set aside.

2 Combine the Miso Dipping Sauce ingredients in a small saucepan and cook, stirring over high heat until sugar dissolves. Set aside to cool before serving.

3 Cut the tofu into 8 equal pieces. Line the bottom of a medium frying pan with the *nori* then carefully arrange the tofu on top.

4 Carefully pour over cold water until tofu is just covered. Place the pan over medium heat and cook for 6–8 minutes or until tofu is heated through. Do not let the water boil or it will break up the tofu.

5 Carefully remove tofu pieces with a slotted spoon and divide between 4 small serving bowls. Discard *nori*. Garnish with the spring onions and grated ginger then serve with the Soy and Miso Dipping Sauces.

Serves 4
Preparation time: **12 mins**
Cooking time: **12 mins**

Braised Daikon

500 g (1 lb) daikon
1 teaspoon *dashi* pow-
   der dissolved in 1 liter
   (4 cups) water or 1 liter
   (4 cups) Dashi Stock
   (see page 5)
2 teaspoons sugar
2 tablespoons soy sauce
4 teaspoons sake
3 tablespoons *mirin*

Serves 4
Preparation time: **10 mins**
Cooking time: **3 hours**

1 Remove skin and thick outer layer and slice the daikon into eight thick pieces. Cut a thin strip on an angle from the top and bottom edge of each piece. Cut a shallow cross into the top on one side.

2 Place the daikon slices in a saucepan with *dashi* mixture or Dashi Stock, sugar, soy sauce and sake. Bring to the boil, removing any impurities from the surface with a spoon. Boil for 10 minutes then reduce heat and simmer covered for $2^1/_2$ hours or until daikon is tender and lightly browned.

3 Gently stir in the *mirin*. Set aside for 10 minutes before serving in small bowls with a little of the cooking liquid.

Daikon and Carrot Salad

450 ml (1³/₄ cups) water
1 tablespoon salt
200 g (1¹/₂ cups) daikon, peeled and cut into matchstick pieces
1 small carrot, peeled and cut into matchstick pieces
3 tablespoons rice wine vinegar
1 tablespoon *mirin*
1 tablespoon soy sauce
1 tablespoon toasted sesame seeds

1 Place 400 ml (1¹/₂ cups) of the water and salt in a medium bowl. Place the daikon and carrot in the salted water for 30 minutes, then drain and set aside.

2 Combine vinegar, remaining water, *mirin* and soy sauce in a small saucepan and bring to a boil over medium heat. Add carrots and daikon and simmer for 1–2 minutes until tender. Remove from the heat and set aside to cool.

3 Place the carrots and daikon between paper towels and squeeze gently to remove excess vinegar. Place in small bowls, sprinkle over sesame seeds and serve.

Serves 4–6
Preparation time: 5 mins + 30 mins soaking time
Cooking time: 5 mins

Vegetable and Soy Stew

8 dried *shiitake* or Chinese mushrooms
90 g (3 oz) burdock root, scraped and cut diagonally
  into thick slices
2 teaspoons rice wine vinegar
$1/_4$ teaspoon salt
130 g ($4^1/_2$ oz) *konnyaku*, cubed (optional)
425 g (14 oz) canned soy beans, drained and rinsed
  well
1 small carrot, peeled and cut into matchstick pieces
2 tablespoons sugar
3 tablespoons *mirin*
4 tablespoons soy sauce

1 Place the mushrooms into a small bowl and add
enough hot water to cover. Set aside for 15 minutes
to reconstitute. Drain the mushrooms and reserve the
liquid. Place the mushrooms between paper towels
and squeeze gently to remove any excess liquid. Cut
into small pieces.
2 Place burdock root into a small bowl and add enough
water to cover. Add vinegar and let stand for 5 minutes. Drain and rinse well.
3 Combine salt and *konnyaku* in a small bowl. Place in
a small saucepan and add enough cold water to cover.
Bring to a boil over high heat and simmer for 5 minutes. Drain and rinse well.
4 Place mushrooms, reserved liquid, burdock,
konnyaku, soybeans and carrots into a medium
saucepan and add enough water to cover. Bring to
a boil, removing any impurities from the surface with
a spoon. Add sugar, *mirin* and half the soy sauce.
Reduce heat to low and simmer for 15 minutes. Add
remaining soy sauce and continue to simmer for
another 15 minutes or until vegetables are tender.
Serve warm or cold.

Serves 4–6
Preparation time: **15 mins**
Cooking time: **35 mins**

Grilled Leeks with Miso and Sesame

1 stalk leek, trimmed
1 tablespoon sesame
  seeds
1 teaspoon red miso
  paste
1 teaspoon sugar
$1/4$ teaspoon *dashi*
  powder dissolved in
  2 teaspoons water
1 teaspoon rice wine
  vinegar
Few sprigs parsley, to
  garnish (optional)

1 Cut the leek into thick slices. Place on an aluminum-lined griller tray and grill under a broiler or over a barbecue grill for 6–8 minutes, turning occasionally, until lightly browned.

2 Meanwhile, place sesame seeds in a food processor or mortar and pestle and grind or pound coarsely. Combine ground sesame seeds, miso paste, sugar, *dashi* mixture and vinegar in a mixing bowl. Divide the leeks into 4 equal portions and place on 4 serving platters. Pour over the sesame sauce and serve warm or cold. Garnish with parsley, if desired.

Serves 4
Preparation time: **10 mins**
Cooking time: **10 mins**

Japanese-style Hamburger Steaks

3 tablespoons bread-
    crumbs
4 tablespoons sake
150 g (5 oz) minced beef
150 g (5 oz) minced pork
    or chicken
3 tablespoons chopped
    leek
1 egg, lightly beaten
1 tablespoon white miso
    paste
$^1/_4$ teaspoon salt
1 teaspoon cracked black
    pepper
2 tablespoons oil
$^1/_2$ tablespoon soy sauce
$1^1/_2$ tablespoons butter
    (about 30 g/1 oz), cubed
Tonkatsu or steak sauce,
    to serve

1 Combine breadcrumbs and 2 tablespoons of the sake in a medium bowl. Add beef and pork or chicken, leek, egg, miso paste, salt and pepper, then mix with a fork until well combined.

2 Wet hands and shape the meat mixture into 4 round patties, each about 2-cm ($^3/_4$-in) thick.

3 Heat a large frying pan over medium heat. Add the oil, heat, then fry the patties for 4-5 minutes on each side. Add remaining 2 tablespoons sake, soy sauce and butter and stir to combine. Remove pan from heat and serve patties drizzled with a little sauce and a side salad of sliced lettuce leaves, parsley, onions and tomatoes, if desired. Top each patty with 1 teaspoon finely grated daikon and *kinome* leaf, if desired. Serve with Tonkatsu or steak sauce, if desired.

Serves 4
Preparation time: 8–10 mins
Cooking time: 12–15 mins

Beef and Asparagus Skewers

8 asparagus spears
300 g (10 oz) steak, cut into 24 very thin, long strips
$^1/_2$ teaspoon salt, adding extra to taste
$^1/_2$ teaspoon pepper, adding extra to taste
1 clove garlic, crushed
1 tablespoon sesame oil
2 teaspoons soy sauce
6 bamboo skewers, soaked in water 30 minutes
1 lemon cut into wedges, to garnish
Japanese mustard to serve

1 Cut off the bottom portions of the asparagus spears.
Blanch the asparagus in a medium saucepan with a bit
of salted water for 1 minute or until just tender and
bright green. Immediately plunge into iced water until
cold. Drain well and pat dry on paper towels. Cut each
asparagus spear into 3 pieces.
2 Season the beef slices with salt and pepper and rub a
little garlic into each slice. Place a piece of asparagus at
the bottom of each beef slice and roll up tightly.
3 Combine sesame oil and soy sauce in a small bowl.
Thread 4 beef rolls onto each skewer and lightly brush
with the sesame oil mixture. Barbecue or broil the beef
skewers for 1–2 minutes on each side or until lightly
browned. Serve with lemon wedges and mustard.

Serves 4
Preparation time: **15 mins**
Cooking time: **10–12 mins**

Stuffed Cabbage Rolls

8 large cabbage leaves
120 g (4 oz) minced beef
120 g (4 oz) minced pork
2 tablespoons chopped
  leek
1 teaspoon grated ginger,
  juice reserved
1 egg, lightly beaten
1 tablespoon potato or
  cornstarch
2 teaspoons + 3 table-
  spoons soy sauce
150 g (5 oz) firm tofu,
  diced
2 teaspoons *dashi* pow-
  der dissolved in $2^1/_2$
  cups (625 ml) water
1 teaspoon sugar
3 tablespoons sake
2 tablespoons *mirin*
2 teaspoons rice wine
  vinegar
Japanese mustard, to
  serve

Serves 4 (makes 8 rolls)
Preparation time: **12 mins**
Cooking time: **30 hours**

1 Remove any thick core parts from the cabbage leaves. Blanch the cabbage leaves in a medium saucepan of boiling salted water for 1 minute or until just tender and a bright green color. Immediately plunge into iced water until cold. Drain and lay flat on a clean paper towel, ribbed side up.

2 In a medium bowl combine the minced beef and pork, leek, ginger, egg, starch, 2 teaspoons of the soy sauce and tofu. Divide mixture into 8 equal portions and place one portion in the center of each cabbage leaf. Fold in the sides and roll up into a neat, firm roll.

3 Line the base of a medium saucepan with the extra cabbage leaf cores and place the cabbage rolls on top, seam side down. Combine *dashi* mixture, sugar, 3 tablespoons of the soy sauce, sake and *mirin* in a medium bowl and carefully pour over cabbage rolls. Place a small plate on top of the rolls so they do not move around during cooking. Cover the saucepan.

4 Bring to a boil then reduce heat and simmer for 15–20 minutes or until rolls are cooked. Remove the saucepan lid, add vinegar and set aside, covered, for 5 minutes. Serve in a shallow serving dish with a little of the cooking liquid, and a side dish of mustard.

Chicken Braised in Sweet Soy (Tori Teriyaki)

4 boneless chicken thighs,
  with skin (about 550 g/
  1¹/₄ lbs)
2 teaspoons + 125 ml
  (¹/₂ cup) sake
2 teaspoons + 3 table-
  spoons soy sauce
3 tablespoons *mirin*
2 teaspoons oil
1 teaspoon grated lemon
  rind, to garnish
  (optional)
1 stalk leek, thinly sliced
  on an angle (optional)

1 Place chicken thighs, 2 teaspoons of sake and 2 teaspoons of soy sauce in a medium bowl and marinate for 30 minutes or overnight. Drain and pat dry on paper towels.

2 Combine *mirin*, 3 tablespoons of soy sauce and ¹/₂ cup of sake in a small bowl and set aside. Heat the oil in a saucepan over medium heat. Fry the chicken thighs for 2–3 minutes on each side or until golden brown. Add the reserved *mirin* mixture, reduce heat to low and cook for 7–8 minutes or until chicken is cooked through and glazed and sauce thickens.

3 Remove from the heat, and serve warm or cold topped with lemon rind and sliced leek, if desired.

Serves 4
Preparation time: 5 mins
  + 30 mins marinating
Cooking time: 15 mins

Fried Chicken Chunks

400 g (14 oz) boneless chicken, cut into bite-sized pieces
3 teaspoons soy sauce
3 teaspoons sake
1 teaspoon sesame oil
4 tablespoons potato or corn starch
Oil for deep-frying
Japanese mustard and mayonnaise, to serve

Serves 4
Preparation time: 10 mins
 + 30 mins marinating
Cooking time: 10 mins

1 Combine the chicken, soy sauce, sake and sesame oil in a medium bowl. Cover and marinate for 30 minutes or overnight. Drain chicken and place in a large plastic bag with the starch. Hold the top of the bag firmly, and shake the chicken pieces until well coated.
2 Heat the oil in a medium saucepan or wok until bubbles just start to form around the handle of a wooden spoon lowered into the oil. Fry the chicken in batches, cooking each batch for 3–4 minutes or until golden brown, turning once.
3 Drain on paper towels and serve with a wedge of lemon and side dishes of mayonnaise and mustard.

Braised Chicken and Lotus Root

8 dried *shiitake* or Chinese mushrooms

1 small fresh lotus root, (about 120 g/5 oz), peeled

2 tablespoons rice wine vinegar

1 medium carrot, peeled

1 tablespoon oil

2 boneless chicken thighs (about 250 g/8 oz), cut into bite-sized pieces

3 tablespoons sake

1 1/2 teaspoons *dashi* powder dissolved in 300 ml (1 1/4 cups) water

2 tablespoons *mirin*

3 tablespoons soy sauce

12 snow peas, tops and tails removed

1 stalk leek, shredded with vegetable peeler, to garnish (optional)

1 Place mushrooms in a small bowl and add enough hot water to cover. Let stand for 15 minutes to reconstitute. Drain the mushrooms and reserve the liquid. Place between paper towels and squeeze gently to remove excess liquid. Cut the stalks off the mushrooms.

2 Cut lotus root in half breadthwise and then slice thinly. Place in a small bowl with vinegar and enough water to cover. Let stand for 10 minutes, then drain.

3 Cut carrot into thin slices at an angle and set aside.

4 Heat the oil in a medium saucepan over high heat. Fry the chicken for 1–2 minutes on each side or until golden brown. Drain and discard any excess oil. Add mushrooms, lotus root, carrot and sake. Stir well. Add *dashi* mixture and bring to the boil removing any impurities from the surface with a spoon or paper towel. Add *mirin* and half of the soy sauce. Cover and boil for 5 minutes.

5 Reduce heat to low and simmer the mixture for another 10 minutes. Add remaining soy sauce and snow peas and simmer, covered, for 5 minutes. Set aside for 5 minutes to cool before serving vegetables in small bowls with a little of the cooking liquid.

Serves 4
Preparation time: 20 mins
Cooking time: 35 mins

Braised Pork in Soy

600 g (1¼ lbs) pork spareribs or belly, skin removed
1 tablespoon *dashi* powder dissolved in 800 ml (3¼ cups) water
⅓ cup sake
5 cm (2 in) ginger, sliced into 3 pieces
½ stalk leek, cut into 3 pieces
4 eggs
3 tablespoons sugar
6 tablespoons soy sauce
1 stalk leek, shredded with a vegetable peeler, to garnish (optional)
Japanese mustard, to serve

Serves 4
Preparation time: **8 mins**
Cooking time:
  1 hour 45 mins

1 Place pork, *dashi* mixture, sake, ginger and leek into a large saucepan. Bring to a boil then reduce heat to low. Cover and simmer for 1 hour or until pork is tender, removing any impurities from the surface with a spoon.
2 Meanwhile, boil the eggs in a separate saucepan for 8–10 minutes. Drain, rinse in cold water to cool, peel and set aside.
3 Remove the saucepan containing the pork from the heat and discard ginger and leek. Remove the pork, cut into bite-sized chunks and return to the saucepan along with the hard-boiled eggs, sugar and half of the soy sauce. Bring to a boil over high heat and reduce heat to low. Cover and simmer for 20 minutes.
4 Add remaining soy sauce and cook for another 15 minutes or until pork is tender. Set aside to cool for 10 minutes before serving in bowls with a little of the cooking liquid. Garnish with the shredded leek and serve with mustard on the side.

Leek and Chicken Skewers

300 g (10 oz) boneless chicken, skin removed
2 stalks leek
2 teaspoons sesame oil
1 tablespoon *mirin*
2 teaspoons soy sauce
8 bamboo skewers, soaked in water 30 minutes
1 lemon, cut into wedges

Sweet Soy Dipping Sauce
2 teaspoons *mirin*
1 tablespoon soy sauce
1 teaspoon sugar

1 Cut the chicken into 24 bite-sized pieces. Combine sesame oil, 1 tablespoon of the *mirin* and 2 teaspoons of the soy sauce in a small bowl and add the chicken pieces. Toss well to coat and marinate for 30 minutes or overnight.
2 Slice the leeks into 24 pieces, approximately $2^1/_2$ cm (1 in) long. Thread 3 pieces of leek and 3 pieces of chicken onto each skewer, alternating.
3 To make the Sweet Soy Dipping Sauce, combine the Sauce ingredients in a small saucepan and stir over medium heat until the sugar dissolves. Remove from heat and pour into 4 small dipping sauce bowls.
4 Grill the skewered leek and chicken under a pre-heated broiler or over a barbecue grill for 5–6 minutes on each side or until browned. Serve with lemon wedges and Sweet Soy Dipping Sauce.

Serves 4 (makes 8 skewers)
Preparation time: **15 mins + 30 mins marinating**
Cooking time: **10–12 mins**

Bacon and Vegetable Pancake (Okonomiyaki)

1 tablespoon oil
2 tablespoons bottled tonkatsu or steak sauce
2 teaspoons dried bonito flakes, to garnish
2 teaspoons dried green seaweed flakes, to garnish
Mayonnaise, to serve (optional)

Pancake Batter
3 eggs, lightly beaten
$^1/_2$ teaspoon *dashi* powder dissolved in 125 ml ($^1/_2$ cup) water
$^2/_3$ cup flour
3 thin slices bacon, chopped
$^1/_2$ cup corn kernels
4 Chinese cabbage leaves, shredded
$^1/_2$ teaspoon salt
$^1/_2$ teaspoon cracked black pepper

1 To prepare the Pancake Batter, combine the eggs and *dashi* mixture in a small bowl. Place flour in a separate bowl and add the egg mixture. Stir until smooth and well combined. Stir in bacon, corn kernels, cabbage, salt and pepper.
2 Heat a frying pan over medium heat. Pour in the oil, heat and add the Pancake Batter. Cook for 3–4 minutes or until golden brown, then carefully turn the Batter over and cook the other side.
3 Cut into 8 wedges and serve with tonkatsu or steak sauce. Sprinkle dried bonito flakes and green seaweed flakes over to taste, and drizzle with a little mayonnaise, if desired.

Serves 4–6
Preparation time: **10 mins**
Cooking time: **8–10 mins**

Pan-fried Fish Fillets

1 tablespoon oil
450 g (1 lb) cod or seabass, cut into fillets
3 tablespoons grated daikon, drained, to garnish
1 tablespoon shredded spring onions, to garnish

Soy Mixture
1 1/2 tablespoons soy sauce
1 1/2 teaspoons sugar
2 tablespoons *mirin*
2 tablespoons sake
2 teaspoons rice wine vinegar
1 teaspoon *dashi* powder dissolved in 80 ml (1/3 cup)
 water
4 thick slices fresh ginger

1 Combine the Soy Mixture ingredients in a small
bowl and set aside.
2 Heat the oil in a large frying pan over medium heat.
Cook the fish fillets for 2–3 minutes on each side or
until lightly browned.
3 Pour over the Soy Mixture, cover and cook over
medium heat for 2 minutes. Reduce heat to low and
cook for another 3 minutes or until fish is tender and
sauce thickens.
4 Discard ginger and serve with grated daikon and
spring onions.

Serves 4
Preparation time: 5 mins
Cooking time: 10 mins

Salt-grilled Fish

4 whole horse mackerel or other small fish
  (about 450 g/1 lb), scaled and washed
2 tablespoons salt
$1/_2$ cup grated daikon, drained
1 lemon cut into wedges
Soy sauce, to serve
4 sprigs *kinome* leaves, to garnish (optional)

1 Using a sharp, small knife remove the hard fin section
near the tail of each fish. Using kitchen scissors remove
the gills from the belly of the fish. Make a slit along
the belly of the fish and carefully remove the innards.
Wash each fish and pat dry with paper towels.
2 Make 2–3 shallow lengthwise slits on both sides of
each fish to ensure even cooking. Rub salt on both
sides of each fish and place under a preheated broiler
or on a barbecue grill. Cook for 4–5 minutes on each
side or until golden brown.
3 Serve each fish with a mound of grated daikon drizzled with a little soy sauce, and lemon wedges.

*Kinome sprigs are used as a garnish in Japanese cui-
sine. They have a minty flavor and may be substituted
with mint leaves.*

Serves 4
Preparation time: **12–15 mins**
Cooking time: **10 mins**

Crispy Prawn, Mushroom and Fish Skewers

4 large prawns (about 200 g/7 oz), peeled and deveined, tails intact
8 fresh *shiitake* mushrooms
4 teaspoons sake
4 teaspoons soy sauce
16 small bamboo skewers
4 small whiting fillets (about 120 g/4 oz) tails intact and trimmed
2 pickled apricots (about 25 g/1 oz), seeds removed and finely chopped
4 fresh shiso or basil leaves
2 eggs
1 tablespoon water
$1/3$ cup flour, adding extra as needed
$1/2$ teaspoon salt
$1/2$ teaspoon pepper
2 cups (120 g/4 oz) fine breadcrumbs, adding extra as needed
Oil for deep-frying
Dark soy sauce, to serve
Japanese mustard, to serve

1 Place prawns and mushrooms in 2 separate bowls. Combine the sake and soy sauce and divide into 2 equal portions. Pour the sake mixture over the prawns and mushrooms and marinate for 30 minutes. Drain and thread prawns onto the skewers through the center so the prawns lie flat and the tail is open at the end. Drain and thread the mushrooms onto a skewer through the center so they lie flat.

2 Wash the whiting fillets and gently pat dry with paper towels. Place skin side down and spread with a little of the chopped pickled apricot. Top with a shiso or basil leaf and gently roll towards the tail. Thread onto a skewer from the tail end making sure the roll is secure.

3 Beat the eggs with water and place in a shallow bowl. Place flour seasoned with salt and pepper on a plate. Place breadcrumbs on another plate. Starting with the mushrooms, coat each skewered food with flour, then dip in beaten egg mixture and coat in breadcrumbs, pressing lightly to get a good coating.

4 Heat the oil in a medium saucepan until bubbles form around the handle of a wooden spoon lowered into the oil. Deep-fry each skewered item for 2–3 minutes or until golden brown. Be careful not to drop the skewers into the oil. Turn occasionally to ensure even browning. Drain on paper towels and serve with a salad of sliced lettuce leaves, parsley and onions, if desired. Serve dark soy sauce and mustard on the side.

Serves 4 (makes 12 skewers)
Preparation time: 10 minutes + 30 mins marinating
Cooking time: 10–12 mins

Soba Noodles in Sweet Soy Broth

1 1/2 tablespoons dried *wakame* seaweed

300 g (10 oz) dried *soba* noodles

4 tablespoons shredded leek

2 tablespoons pickled ginger

4 eggs (optional)

1/4 cup sugar, or to taste

1 cup (250 ml) *mirin*

5 teaspoons *dashi* powder dissolved in 4 cups (1 liter) water

1/2 cup (125 ml) soy sauce

Japanese seven-spice pepper powder (optional)

1 Soak seaweed in cold water for 5 minutes or until reconstituted. Drain and set aside.

2 Cook noodles according to package instructions. Drain and rinse well in cold water to remove excess surface starch. Divide between 4 medium bowls.

3 Divide the reserved seaweed, leek and pickled ginger in equal portions between the 4 bowls, arrange on top of noodles and crack an egg carefully into the center of each bowl if desired.

4 Combine sugar and *mirin* in a saucepan over medium heat and stir until sugar dissolves. Add *dashi* mixture and soy sauce, stir and bring to the boil. Pour immediately over noodles and serve sprinkled with seven-spice pepper powder, if desired.

Serves 4
Preparation time: 10 mins
Cooking time: 10 mins

Udon Noodle Soup with Prawn and Vegetable Tempura

4 medium prawns (about 170 g/6 oz), peeled and deveined

1 bunch *enoki* mushrooms, roots removed, mushrooms separated

4 sprigs *mitsuba* or chervil leaves, adding extra to garnish

$1/2$ small carrot peeled and cut into matchstick pieces

2 tablespoons flour

Tempura Batter (see page 5)

Oil for deep-frying

$1 1/2$ tablespoons dried *wakame* seaweed

4 tablespoons shredded leek

250 g (8 oz) dried *udon* noodles

3 tablespoons sugar

$1 1/3$ cups (330 ml) *mirin*

2 tablespoons *dashi* powder dissolved in 5 cups ($1 1/4$ liters) water

$1/2$ cup (125 ml) soy sauce

1 Roughly chop prawns and place in a medium bowl with mushrooms, *mitsuba* and carrots. Sprinkle the flour and toss to combine. Add the Tempura Batter, to the prawn mixture and toss to coat lightly.

2 Heat the oil in a medium saucepan or wok, until bubbles form around the handle of a wooden spoon lowered into the oil.

3 Divide the prawn mixture into 4 equal portions. Using a large spoon drop one portion into the hot oil and use the spoon to hold it to the side of the saucepan until the batter starts to cook and the fritter remains in one piece. Cook for 2–3 minutes or until lightly browned. Drain on paper towels, and repeat with remaining portions.

4 Soak seaweed in cold water for 5 minutes or until reconstituted. Drain and set aside. Cook the noodles according to the package instructions. Drain and rinse well in cold water to remove excess surface starch. Divide the noodles between 4 medium bowls. Divide seaweed and shredded leek into 4 equal portions and arrange on top of noodles with a fritter.

5 Combine sugar, *mirin*, *dashi* mixture and soy sauce in a medium saucepan over high heat and bring to the boil. Pour immediately over noodles and serve.

Serves 4
Preparation time: 20 mins
Cooking time: **15–17 mins**

Stir-fried Soba Noodles

300 g (10 oz) dried *soba* noodles

1 carrot, peeled and cut into matchstick pieces

2 tablespoons sesame oil

$1/2$ small onion, cut into thin wedges

100 g ($3^1/_2$ oz) pork, finely sliced

1 green capsicum, seeded and sliced

1 clove garlic, finely chopped

2 cups sliced cabbage

2 tablespoons sake

1 tablespoon soy sauce

5 tablespoons tonkatsu or steak sauce

4 tablespoons pickled ginger, to garnish

Dried green seaweed flakes, to garnish

Dried bonito flakes, to garnish

1 Cook noodles according to the package instructions. Drain and rinse well in cold water to remove excess starch.

2 Heat the oil in a large frying pan or wok over high heat. Add the onions and carrots and stir-fry for 2 minutes or until onions are transparent. Add pork and capsicum and stir-fry another 2 minutes. Add garlic and cabbage and stir-fry for another 2 minutes or until cabbage starts to wilt. Add noodles, sake and soy sauce and stir-fry until noodles are heated through.

3 Stir in the tonkatsu or steak sauce and serve hot. Garnish with pickled ginger, green seaweed flakes and dried bonito flakes.

The pork must be cut in very thin slices, approximately 1 mm thick. To do this, partially freeze the meat for 15–20 minutes, then slice carefully with a sharp knife.

Serves 4
Preparation time: **10–12mins**
Cooking time: **18–20 mins**

Rice Patties with Tuna and Spring Onions

1 cup uncooked Japanese rice
400 ml (1$^1/_2$ cups) water
2 sheets *nori*

Spring Onion Filling
4 teaspoons finely chopped spring onions
2 tablespoons white miso paste
$^1/_4$ teaspoon Japanese seven-spice pepper powder
1 teaspoon sesame oil

Tuna Filling
3 tablespoons drained canned tuna
2 teaspoons Japanese mayonnaise
$^1/_2$ teaspoon white miso paste

Makes 4 large portions
Preparation time: **15 mins**
Cooking time: **30 mins**

1 Wash the rice and place in a rice cooker or large saucepan with water. Cook the rice in the rice cooker, or cover saucepan with a tight-fitting lid and bring to a boil. Reduce heat to low and simmer rice, covered, for 20–25 minutes or until cooked. Rice is cooked when small steam holes are visible on the surface of the rice.

2 To make the Spring Onion Filling, combine the spring onions, miso paste, seven-spice pepper powder and the sesame oil in a bowl to form a paste. Divide the Filling into 2 equal portions.

3 To make the Tuna Filling, combine the tuna, mayonnaise and miso paste in a separate bowl. Divide the Filling into 2 equal portions.

4 Divide the rice into 4 equal portions. Wet your hands then form each portion of rice into a ball and make a deep hole in the center with your finger. Fill 2 of the rice balls with the Spring Onion Filling and 2 of the rice balls with the Tuna Filling. Carefully shape each rice ball into a triangle, making sure to enclose the filling.

4 Cut the *nori* sheets lengthwise into strips large enough to encase each rice triangle. Stand the flat end of the rice triangle in the center of each *nori* piece as shown. Lift both sides of each *nori* sheet to wrap each rice triangle and serve.

Sprinkle water on your hands so the rice does not stick to them.

Make a hole in the center of the rice ball with your finger then add a portion of the Filling.

Carefully shape rice into a triangle, making sure to enclose the filling.

Stand the flat end of the rice triangle in the center of each strip of nori.

Grilled Salmon with Rice and Green Tea

4 tablespoons shredded leek

1 cup uncooked Japanese rice

400 ml (1 1/2 cups) water

200 g (7 oz) fresh salmon fillets, washed and trimmed if needed

1 tablespoon *dashi* powder

1 tablespoon *mirin*

3 teaspoons soy sauce

2 sheets *nori*, cut into thin strips

1 tablespoon toasted white sesame seeds

1 liter (4 cups) hot water mixed with 4 teaspoons green tea powder or 2 green tea bags

1 Soak the leeks in a small bowl of water for 10 minutes. Drain well.

2 Wash the rice and place in a rice cooker with the water and cook. Alternatively, place the rice and water in a saucepan, cover with a tight fitting lid and bring to a boil. Reduce heat to low and simmer covered for 20–25 minutes or until cooked. The rice is cooked when small steam holes are visible on the surface of the rice.

3 Place the salmon, *dashi* powder, *mirin* and soy sauce in a bowl. Toss well then marinate for 30 minutes. Place on a lightly greased, aluminum-lined grilling tray. Grill each side of the salmon under a preheated broiler for 3–4 minutes on medium heat or until cooked through. Cool and flake with a fork. Divide rice between 4 medium bowls.

4 Divide salmon, *nori* and leek between each bowl and gently pour over hot green tea. Sprinkle with sesame seeds and serve immediately.

Serves 4
Preparation time: **5 mins + 30 mins marinating time**
Cooking time: **25 mins**

Pork Cutlets with Egg on Rice (Tonkatsudon)

$^1/_3$ cup flour, adding
extra as needed
$^1/_2$ teaspoon salt
$^1/_2$ teaspoon pepper
2 cups breadcrumbs,
adding extra as needed
4 pork cutlets (about
550 g/1$^1/_4$ lbs)
80 ml ($^1/_3$ cup) milk
Oil for deep-frying
1 teaspoon *dashi* pow-
der dissolved in 250 ml
(1 cup) water
60 ml ($^1/_4$ cup) soy
sauce
3 tablespoons *mirin*
3 tablespoons sugar
2 tablespoons oil
2 medium onions,
halved and sliced
6 eggs, lightly beaten
taking care not to froth
5 cups freshly cooked
Japanese rice
1 sheet *nori*, sliced into
thin strips, to garnish
Red pickled ginger, to
garnish

1 On two separate plates, place flour seasoned with salt and pepper, and breadcrumbs. Coat each pork cutlet with flour, dip in milk and coat in breadcrumbs, pressing lightly to coat well.

2 Heat the oil in a medium saucepan or wok over medium heat, until bubbles just start to form around the handle of a wooden spoon lowered into the oil. Fry pork in 2 batches for 4–5 minutes or until golden brown and tender. Drain on paper towels and cut each steak into thick slices, keeping each portion together.

3 Combine *dashi* mixture, soy sauce, *mirin* and sugar in a medium saucepan. Bring to the boil then remove from the heat.

4 Heat a large frying pan over medium heat. Add 2 tablespoons of oil and the onions, and cook for 3 minutes or until soft and transparent. Spread onions evenly over the base of the frying pan and carefully place each portion of crumbed pork on top. Pour over the *dashi* mixture and cook for 1 minute. Pour eggs over a pair of chopsticks and stir lightly to combine with the *dashi* mixture. Cover and cook for 2 minutes or until egg is slightly wet.

5 Slide each portion of the crumbed pork out of the saucepan onto a bowl of rice and garnish with the *nori* and pickled ginger.

Serves 4
Preparation time: **12 mins**
Cooking time: **20 mins**

Tempura and Rice with Broth

4 large fresh prawns
(about 200 g/7 oz),
peeled and deveined,
tails intact
1 teaspoon sake
Oil for deep-frying
4 medium chunks
unpeeled pumpkin
(about 150 g/5 oz)
8 fresh *shiitake* mush-
rooms, stems removed
1 Japanese eggplant
(about 150 g/5 oz),
trimmed and thinly
sliced lengthwise
3 tablespoons flour
Tempura Batter (see
page 5)
5 cups cooked Japanese
rice

Broth

$1/4$ teaspoon *dashi* powder dissolved in 200 ml
($3/4$ cup) water
2 tablespoons soy sauce
2 tablespoons *mirin*
2 tablespoons grated
daikon

1 To make the Broth, combine the *dashi* mixture, soy
sauce and *mirin* in a medium saucepan. Bring to the
boil then remove from heat and stir in the grated
daikon. Set aside and keep warm.

2 Make 3–4 slits along the underside of each prawn to
prevent it curling when fried. Place into a small bowl
with sake and marinate for 10 minutes.

3 Heat oil to 180°C (350°F) in a medium saucepan or
until bubbles form around the handle of a wooden
spoon lowered into the oil.

4 Coat the pumpkin, mushrooms, eggplant and prawns
with flour then dip into the Tempura Batter and fry
for 2–3 minutes turning once, or until very lightly
colored, cooking prawns last. Drain on paper towels.

5 Divide rice between 4 medium bowls and top with
the fried vegetables and prawns. Pour over a little of
the Broth mixture and serve.

Serves 4
Preparation time: **25 mins**
Cooking time: **15 mins**

Sweet Red Beans with Jelly

4 teaspoons powdered gelatin or 20 g ($^1/_2$ oz) agar-agar (*kanten*)
250 ml (1 cup) hot water
4 tablespoons sugar
375 ml (1$^1/_2$ cups) cold water
200 g (7 oz) canned azuki beans
400 g (13 oz) sliced peaches or mixed fruit
125 ml ($^1/_2$ cup) water
1 tablespoon glucose syrup
4 maraschino or glace cherries, to garnish (optional)
Few sprigs *mitsuba* leaves, to garnish (optional)

1 Sprinkle the gelatin or agar-agar over the hot water and stir until dissolved. Add the sugar and stir until dissolved. Strain into a medium bowl and add 250 ml (1 cup) of cold water.

2 Pour the gelatin or agar-agar mixture into a 16 x 20 cm (6$^1/_2$ x 8 in) shallow cake pan lined with plastic wrap. Refrigerate for 4 hours or until set. Turn out onto a plastic cutting board and cut into 1-cm ($^1/_2$-in) cubes.

3 Place remaining 125 ml ($^1/_2$ cup) cold water, and glucose syrup in a small saucepan and heat over high heat. Stir continuously until glucose syrup dissolves and bring to the boil. Reduce heat to low and simmer for 10 minutes. Remove syrup from the heat and set aside to cool.

4 Heat azuki beans in a small saucepan over medium heat until just heated through. Remove from heat and set aside. Place a spoonful of azuki beans into 4 parfait or dessert glasses.

5 Divide the jelly cubes and fruit between the 4 glasses and top with remaining azuki beans. Pour the syrup over to serve. Top with a cherry and *mitsuba* leaves, if desired.

Serves 6–8
Preparation time: 10 mins + 4 hours for setting jelly
Cooking time: 10–15 mins

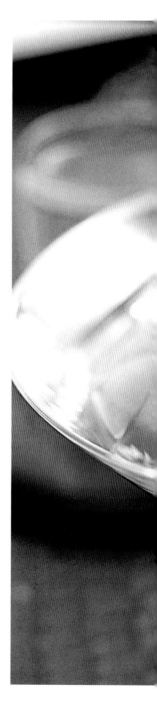

Toffee Plums

8 medium pickled Japanese plums
80 ml (¹/₃ cup) water
1 cup sugar
1 teaspoon rice wine vinegar
8 small bamboo skewers
Few sprigs *mitsuba* leaves to garnish

1 Wash the plums under cold water and pat dry on paper towels. The plums should be very dry and free from any pickling liquid, otherwise the toffee will not stick to the plums. Press a bamboo skewer into the base of each plum then set aside.
2 Place water, sugar and rice wine vinegar in a small saucepan over high heat. Stir continuously until sugar dissolves and bring to the boil. Reduce heat to low and simmer for about 10–15 minutes or until toffee starts to color a little and thicken.
3 Place saucepan into a sink filled with a little cold water for 30 seconds or until the bubbles just subside.
4 Working quickly, dip a skewered plum into the toffee and swirl it around in the toffee to coat. Remove and place on a sheet of baking paper or lightly greased aluminum foil. Repeat with remaining plums.
5 Divide the toffee equally between 8 tall glasses and set aside. When toffee is almost set, place a skewered plum in each glass of toffee and set aside until the toffee sets.

Serves 8
Preparation time: 10 mins
Cooking time: 25 mins

List of Recipes